DIVINE DISTINCTION

The Ministry of the Apostle
The Office of the Bishop

A Position Statement

By

Bishop Ralph L. Dennis

xulon
PRESS

Copyright © 2004 by Ralph L. Dennis Ministries

Requests for information should be addressed to:
Ralph L. Dennis Ministries
6419 York Road Baltimore, MD 21212

Divine Distinction
by Ralph L. Dennis Ministries

Printed in the United States of America

ISBN 1-594676-03-8

Quotes taken from:

Catholic Catechism
Hayden, W.C. Church Polity
Shaff's Bible Dictionary
Vine, W. E. Expository Dictionary, 1997 Thomas Nelson Publisher.

Unless otherwise indicated, Bible quotations are taken from the King James Version. Copyright © 1986 by World Bible Publishers.

www.xulonpress.com

Table of Contents

Preface

*I*t's very important as we embrace this significant subject (Apostles and Bishops in the New Testament) and attempt to present a position statement that is biblically sound, that we do so with the utmost sensitivity. To approach this kind of discussion with preconceived notions and closed minds, could put at- risk those who trust our input for divine direction. Correct interpretation of the Scriptures, not history, must be what we trust as the order of God. Church history has not always demonstrated the will of God. Where it does, it can be used as a divine pattern; where it does not, it must be replaced with the truth of God, even if it presents the challenge of accepting something different from our traditions.

INTRODUCTION:

EARLY CHURCH HISTORY

Early Church History

Very soon after Christ's ascension into heaven, many churches began to appear. In the New Testament, the word church means an assembly or body of people. Christian churches are assemblies or bodies of people who profess to believe that Christ is the Son of God and offers salvation freely from the punishment of sin.

The first Christian church was in Jerusalem. Undoubtedly most, if not all, the members were Jews who accepted Jesus Christ as the Messiah. As Apostles and others spread the good news of salvation through Christ to other cities, the first to hear were generally the Jews. Believers in these other cities also assembled as bodies, just as Christ commanded.

The question of the precise relationship of Judaism to Christianity naturally arose. The Apostles and others began to carry the gospel of Christ to non-Jews, to Gentiles, just as Christ clearly commanded. Soon churches consisting of Jews and Gentiles appeared around the Roman Empire. Some churches came to be totally Gentile. Some Jewish Christians believed that Gentile converts should practice all activities prescribed for Jews by the Law of the Old Testament. But Paul and others denied this. To settle this issue, a meeting was held in Jerusalem to discuss the matter. Christians naturally respected the world's first Christian church whose members were apostles and looked to Jerusalem for guidance.

The Apostles and the elders of the Jerusalem church debated and reached an agreement after James quoted Scripture from the Old Testament. A letter went out from the Jerusalem church to churches in Antioch, Syria, and Cilicia, summarizing the results of the debate. In brief, they said that Gentile Christians did not have to practice all the Jewish laws of the Old Testament (Acts 15:1-33).

CHURCH INDEPENDENCE

The first churches were independent and self-governing in that no one church gave orders to the others. Whatever special respect that was paid to the Jerusalem church soon ended. Christians and unconverted Jews grew further and further apart after the Christians in Jerusalem refused to take part in violent revolts against Roman rule in Jerusalem. The Romans destroyed Jerusalem in 70 A.D., just as Christ had foretold (Luke 21:20-24). The Jewish people would not be independent in their homeland again until the twentieth century (1948).

These early churches had many leaders. Some were called deacons (from the Greek word meaning "servant'). Others were called elders (the Greek word for elder is "presbuteros" which is also the source of the word priest), or bishops (from the Greek word meaning "overseer" or "superintendent"). Some churches had more than one bishop. Some, perhaps all, of the early churches used elder and bishop to refer to the same office (Titus 1:5-7).

The New Testament, while certainly not condoning the absence of leadership, order, and discipline in churches (I Timothy 5:17-19; I Peter 5:1-5; Hebrews 13:7, 17), does not state that any person be all-powerful in any one church or group of churches. The Bible makes Christ the true Head of the Church. Of course, as long as the Apostles lived, the churches had the benefit of special leaders appointed directly by Christ Himself, authorized to speak and act in the name of Christ. The churches recognized this apostolic authority.

WORSHIP PRACTICES

The worship practices of the early churches were very simple. Prior to the 4th century, they did not build special buildings for worship. However, some homes were remodeled for that purpose. Scriptures were read, at first from the Old Testament, and then from parts of the New Testament as it was written. Leaders probably read aloud letters from apostles to the churches. Preachers delivered sermons based on the Scripture and congregations prayed and sang. Songs included Psalms from the Old Testament as well as new hymns. Believers who had received salvation followed Christ in baptism, and churches frequently celebrated the Lord's Supper in remembrance of Christ.

More than once, Paul had to point out mistakes to the churches, such as allowing more than one person to speak at a time. Some leaders were domineering. While no local church has ever been perfect, the New Testament, if read carefully, does reveal clear guidelines for having good churches. In totality, the guidelines, provided by the New Testament, form the ideal New Testament church.

THE INVISIBLE AND VISIBLE CATHOLIC CHURCH

Even though there are many local churches, as God looks down from heaven He sees one church made up of all true Christians. This one great "invisible" church that only God sees can never meet in the way that a local church does. Another name for this one great "invisible" church is catholic, which originally meant "universal" or "one."

The idea of a catholic church gradually separated from the New Testament idea of the "invisible" church and came to mean a single, visible, large, organized church for all Christians. Perhaps the motives were at first seemingly innocent, a desire to unite all Christians (Christ had taught the goodness of unity) and to defend Christian beliefs against distortions, but the visible catholic church soon began to distort Christianity.

Having a single, visible, large, organized church necessitated establishing official relationships between local churches. In all organizations, some give orders and others take them. Organization of the Catholic Church eventuated in dominance of one local church over others.

RESPECT FOR THE CHURCH OF ROME

Before the end of the second century, many Christians began treating the Church of Rome with great respect, just as they had the Jerusalem church earlier. This was only natural, since the city of Rome was the single most important city in the Roman Empire. Even Paul thought very highly of the Church of Rome, as his letter to the Romans in the New Testament states. But there is no record of Paul ever saying what Ireneaus (a church leader in Gaul who wrote around 175 AD) said: that every church had to agree with the Church of Rome.

Ireneaus maintained the supremacy of the Church of Rome and justified the supremacy of bishops through the idea of "Apostolic Succession." The doctrine of apostolic succession asserts that "in order that the full and living Gospel might always be preserved in the Church, the Apostles left bishops as their successors. They gave them their own position of teaching authority. The apostolic preaching which is expressed in a special way in the inspired books, was to be preserved in a continuous line of succession until the end of time" (Catechism of the Catholic Church, Section 1, Chapter 2, Article 2 Paragraph 77).

Likewise, Ireneaus said that the Apostles were "guardians of the gospel." Instead of emphasizing the New Testament as the Christians' permanent linkage to the Apostles, Ireneaus claimed that the Apostles had appointed bishops as their successors and that these successors of Apostles had in turn appointed "successors of successors" of Apostles. The authority of the Apostles had therefore been passed down in an unbroken line to the bishops of his day. He believed that Peter and Paul had found this church; therefore, he naturally held that these two Apostles had appointed the first bishop of Rome.

Peter's role in the "Apostolic Succession" eventually received great emphasis. Peter appears to have been the leader of the Apostles after Christ's ascension into heaven. The New Testament records that Jesus once said to Peter, whose name means "rock," "...thou art Peter, and upon this rock I will build my church; and the gates of hell shall not prevail against it. And I will give thee the keys to the kingdom of heaven; and whatever thou shalt bind on earth shall be bound in heaven; and whatsoever thou shalt loose on earth shall be loosed in heaven" (Matthew 16:18-19). When Christ referred to Peter as the church's foundation, He was speaking of Peter's confession of faith in Him as the Son of God. Christ is The Rock.

During the fifth century, beginning with Leo I, bishops of Rome began using this Scripture to support the Petrine Theory. This theory states that Christ made Peter the head of the Catholic Church and that Peter passed this power to the bishops of Rome, the first of whom he appointed. Yet, the Bible never shows Peter acting as if he were "head" of "the church." Peter himself warned against pastors lording over others rather than being good examples (I Peter 5:1-30).

The Petrine Theory permitted the ideas of the supremacy of the Church of Rome and of the office of the bishop to emerge. The result was the idea of the Roman Catholic Church in which the bishop of the Church of Rome was supreme over all churches. During this time, bishops had come to the forefront. Beginning in the early second century, the general pattern was for a single bishop to be the ruler, the virtual king of each church.

Though initially called Pope ("papa" or "father"), the bishop of the Church of Rome eventually began to rule the Roman Catholic Church as supreme ruler or king. As in other human organizations, the quest for extreme unity in the church easily led to one-man rule or to kings, for the greatest degree of unity. Reminiscent of the old Israelite demand for a human king rather than God, Christians also sought after a human king rather than Christ. Peter's great concern that the shepherds of Christian flocks would act as "lords over God's heritage" rather than "examples to the flock" had come to pass (I Peter 5:3).

The Bible lends no support to Ireneaus' opinions. He claimed that the Roman church had been founded by Peter and Paul, but the New Testament does not say that Peter ever visited Rome. Additionally, the Scriptures do not say that the Apostles passed on their unique authority to others. Instead, the Apostles wrote the New Testament, so that the churches had the Word of God as the true authority.

There is no line of succession with today's apostles and The Twelve. Succession does not validate the ministry of a modern day apostle. The validation rests in the apostle's adherence to the doctrine set forth by the Twelve and the embracing of his responsibility in establishing the Church.

THE ASCENSION GIFT

MINISTRIES

The Ascension Gift Ministries

*T*he Epistle of the Ephesians, called "The Epistle of the Church, the Body of Christ" speaks of five ministries that are given to the Body for a specific time and a specific purpose.

"When He ascended up on high, He led captivity captive, and gave gifts unto men...And He gave some, apostles; and some, prophets; and some, evangelists; and some, pastors and teachers; for the perfecting of the saints, for the work of ministry, for the edifying of the body of Christ: Till we all come in the unity of the faith, and of the knowledge of the Son of God, unto a perfect man, unto the measure of the fullness of Christ..." (Ephesians 4:8, 11-13).

There are some important points to be noted before proceeding to a more detailed study of any of these ministries. What I believe we will find is that we cannot treat one of these gift ministries any differently than we treat another.

THE GODHEAD INVOLVED

In the building and operation of the Church, the Godhead (Father, Son and Holy Spirit) is involved. God is a giving God, and all the power and fullness of the Godhead is made available to the people of God to bring the Church to all that God intends for it to be.

1. The Father God

   The Father gave His Son to be Head over all things (Ephesians 1: 20-22) and to be the Savior of the world (John 3:16; II Corinthians 5: 18, 19). Love motivated the Father to give all in His blessed Son. The Father's burden was the whole world and His gift was His only begotten Son. It is the Father God who gives the power to operate and work all things in the Body of Christ. It is God that "worketh all in all" (I Corthinians 12:6).

2. The Son of God

   The Son of God gave Himself for the Church (Ephesians 5:23-27). He prayed not for the world, but for His own (John 17:9). The burden of the Son was for a glorious Church. The Son not only gave Himself, but He also gave the Holy Spirit (Acts 5: 32; John 16) and ministry-gifts to perfect the Church. After His death, burial, resurrection, ascension and glorification, He gave the five gift ministries mentioned in Ephesians 4: 9-11. These ministries are actually expressions of Himself. Through these, His own ministry flows into the many-membered Body of Christ, the Church. Because they were given after the ascension, they are called "post ascension gift ministries" (I Corinthians 12:5; Ephesians 4: 8-16).

These are His instruments for the perfecting of the Church in earth. Thus, the Son's burden is the whole Church. The Son's gifts to the Church are the Holy Spirit and the five ascension gift ministries.

3. The Holy Spirit

   The Holy Spirit is God's gift through Christ to believers individually and to the Church corporately. He works with the Father and with the Son. He also is a giver of gifts. He gives the spiritual gifts mentioned in I Corinthians 12: 4, 7.

Thus, we have "diversities of gifts, but the same Spirit-" The Holy Spirit. And we have "differences of ministries, but the same Lord-" the Son. And we have "diversities of operations, but the same God-" the Father.

The burden of the Holy Spirit is both the individual believer, and the whole Body of Christ, the Church. He desires that all flow in their place and function in the Body. Thus, the Father, Son and Holy Spirit (the eternal Godhead) are vitally involved in the eternal purpose concerning the Church.

ASCENSION- GIFT MINISTRIES

It was AFTER Christ's descending and ascending ministry that He gave these gifts to the Church. A number of scriptures speak of Christ's "descending and ascending" to earth and heaven (Genesis 28:12; Proverbs 30:4; Romans 10:6, 7; John 3:13; Ephesians 4: 1-16).

He descended from heaven to earth to redeem us. He ascended from earth to heaven to glorify us. The five ministry gifts were given for this purpose also. It is worth noting that Christ did not choose a prophet, evangelist, pastor or teacher of the fivefold type BEFORE His ascension. He chose TWELVE APOSTLES AS THE FOUNDATION of the New Testament Church. Thus, these five are "post-ascension ministries."

THE GIFTS OF GRACE

There are five ascension gift ministries. Five is the number in Scripture that God associates with grace, atonement, and life. It is in and through these five gifts that the Lord's power, grace, life and truths of the atonement flow.

They are "grace gifts" (Ephesians 4: 7, 11; Romans 12: 3, 6), from the risen Christ. They are His gifts to the Church which are expressions and channels of His grace. Paul received "grace and apostleship" (Romans 1:5; I Corinthians 3:10; Romans 15:15, 16;

Galatians 2:9; I Corinthians 15: 9, 10).

The grace of Christ flows through these gifts. We may say that each of these ministries is an expression of Christ, "Christ in you, the hope of glory" (Colossians 1:27):

* The fruit of the Spirit - His nature and character
* The gifts of the Spirit - His power
* The ministry gifts - His offices

Christ gives Himself back to the Church through His ministries. Because He is the fullness of the Godhead bodily, He flows into the many-membered Body of Christ which is His visible expression in the earth (Colossians 1:19; 2:9; John 1: 14-16). Thus "of His fullness have all we received grace for grace."

THE FIVEFOLD MINISTRY

The ministries specified are the Apostle, Prophet, Evangelist, Pastor and Teacher (Ephesians 4:11). These we also call governmental or headship ministries, because of the responsibility, accountability and authority placed on them by God.

In regard to the New Testament Church, there are about 81 references to Apostles; 14 references to Prophets; 10 references to Teachers (though Scribe is mentioned many times, 47 times, meaning Master); 3 references to Evangelists; 1 reference to Pastor, plus about 16 to Shepherd (same Greek word).

THE PURPOSE OF THE FIVEFOLD MINISTRY

The purpose for which these five ascension-gift ministries are given is seen clearly in Ephesians 4:12 :

1. **FOR** the perfecting or maturing of the saints,
2. **FOR** the work of the ministry, i.e. to bring the saints into the work of their ministry,

3. **FOR** the edifying or building up of the Body of Christ.

We may also say that these five ministries are given to balance each other, as well as, to bring balance in the Body of Christ.

THE CONSUMMATE MINISTRY OF THE ASCENSION GIFTS

The end result of these ministry gifts is found in Ephesians 4:13-16:

1. **TO BRING** the Church to the unity of the faith, unto the knowledge of the Son of God.

2. **TO BRING** the Church unto a perfect man, a full grown man, maturity.

3. **TO BRING** the Church unto the measure of the stature of the fullness of Christ.

Having arrived at that standard the Lord will be able to" present to Himself a glorious Church, without spot or wrinkle, holy and without blemish" (Ephesians 5:23-33).

TIME LIMIT

We may ask what is the time limit or duration of these five ministry gifts. These ministries are given UNTIL the purpose is accomplished as laid out in Ephesians 4:12-16. The fivefold ministry has not always been accepted by the Church as a whole. The ministries of Evangelist, Pastor, and Teacher have generally been accepted. However, the ministries of Apostle and Prophet have been relegated to the past history of the Church- its foundation and its inception.

However, the Word says that these five ministries were given by

Christ until the consummation. This has not yet been reached. Therefore, there remains the necessity for all of the fivefold ascension gift ministries. Each has a part to play in the whole of the purpose of God.

THE MINISTRY

OF THE APOSTLE

The Ministry of the Apostle

When Jesus ascended on high, He did not abandon the infant Church. Jesus told the disciples that it was to their advantage for Him to go away. His departure would hasten the release of the Holy Spirit (John 16:7-16). As long as Jesus was here on earth the body of Christ was confined to the human limitation of space and time; Jesus could only be in one place at one time. When Jesus was on earth, He was the fountainhead of all ministries. He was the apostle, prophet, evangelist, pastor, teacher, shower of mercy, intercessor, ruler, deacon, exhorter and giver- all wrapped up into one. He had the fullness of all ministries. However, it was Jesus' desire that this ministry of life and healing be taken to the uttermost parts of the earth.

Once He ascended, He received of the Father the gift of the Holy Spirit, and in Acts 2, the disciples of the Lord were endued with power from on high. He made it possible for his ministry to reach the four corners of the earth. With this endowment, God gave a visible sign of what was taking place in the heavenlies in regard to the ministry of the body of Christ. A careful study of the Greek text in Acts 2, indicates that there was a visible manifestation of a fire that separated, distributed itself, and came to rest on each of them. The thought implies a singular flame that was dissipated as a part of that flame rested on each one present.

This is in essence what Jesus did with His ministry. When He ascended, He broke down His fullness of ministry into smaller measures and distributed these measures until the whole was invested. So He gave some apostles, some prophets, some evangelists, and pastors and teachers. He did not give the whole to anyone, but He gave each a measure of the gift of Christ. In this way, Christ continues to carry on His prophetic ministry through the prophets He has set in the body. He continues to carry on His teaching ministry through the teachers that He has called and equipped in the body, and so on.

Some, however, have been given ministries that relate to authority in the body. Some, Christ has given to oversee the function of the body and how the members of the body relate to each other. Some, Christ has given as builders to make sure that every member is functioning in the unique place for which God has designed him. In Ephesians 4, it tells us that these ministries are for the adjusting or the equipping of the saints to do their service and they are for the building up of the body of Christ. The first of the fivefold ministry is the apostle.

THE DEFINITION OF TERMS

In order to get a clear understanding of the ministry of the Apostle in the New Testament, we must carefully look at the origin and use of this word. Both the name and the ministry of the apostle have been frequently surrounded by a halo. For this reason, people have been somewhat reluctant to apply these terms to people. Yet, if we could understand some distinctions that exist between apostles and the actual function of the apostle, it would perhaps once again release this ministry with power to the body of Christ.

The word "apostle" (Greek- apostolos) literally means "one who is sent forth." This definition in itself, however, does not really help us because it is too general. All ministries should, in a sense, be sent forth. Why is this term singled out by Jesus and applied to a certain kind of ministry in His day? Perhaps the key for this lies not in the definition of the word itself, but in the use of the word in the classical Greek world, where it was used to refer to four things:

1. an emissary or ambassador;
2. a fleet of ships or an expedition sent with a specific objective;
3. the admiral who commanded the fleet;
4. the colony which was founded by the admiral.

If a fleet of ships left Rome with the purpose of establishing a new colony, all of these were called apostles - the fleet, the admiral, and the new found colony.

The particular truth that is emphasized by this usage is the relationship of those who were sent by the sender. All of these, the admiral, the fleet, and the colony that was formed, represented a true image of the one by whom they were sent. In other words, they were faithful to transmit or reflect the intentions of the sender (Hebrews 3:1). The primary attitude of a true apostle, must be faithfulness. This association and connection between the sender and the one who is sent is clearly seen in the New Testament. There is an old Jewish maxim that teaches "the apostle is the equivalent to him who has sent him." This is not seen as simply a matter of substitution, but rather, the one who commissions is seen to be present in the person. This is seen most vividly in the life of Jesus, who was the great Apostle sent from the Father to establish a Church and faithfully represent the intentions of the Father (Luke 10:18; John 13:16). "He that receiveth you receiveth me, and he that receiveth me receiveth him that sent me" (Matthew 10:40).

In the light of all of this, how significant it was for Jesus, after spending the night in prayer, to take twelve of his disciples and name them "apostles" (Luke 6:13). These were going to be ambassadors or emissaries of Jesus. They were going to go out under orders to establish a new colony, the Church, which would truly reflect the intentions of the sender. It would be a true representation of the Heavenly City with foundations whose builder and maker is God. It would be a little bit of heaven on earth and it would be known as the faithful city (Isaiah 1:26). An apostle then, is one who is sent forth with authority, who faithfully represents the purpose and the intentions of the sender.

THE LEVELS OF APOSTLES IN THE NEW TESTAMENT

The New Testament makes a distinction between several classes of apostles. Two of these classes (Jesus and the Twelve Apostles) are no longer operating directly in the church; however, their influence forms the basis for everything else that happened. There are **four** main levels of the apostolic ministry.

1. **Jesus Christ** - Jesus Christ was and is the Chief Apostle (Hebrew 3:1). He was sent by the Father from heaven to accomplish the divine intention (John 3:16; 20:21). Jesus was absolutely faithful to represent His Father to us (John 4:34; 5:19, 30; 6:38; 8: 28-29, 42; 12:44, 45).

2. **The Twelve Apostles of The Lamb** –This is a distinct group specifically chosen and commissioned by Christ in His earthly ministry after a night of prayer (Luke 6:12). These are referred to as the apostles of the Lamb and have a unique place for all eternity, their names being recorded in the twelve foundations of the holy city (Rev. 21:14). These twelve marked the beginning of a new age in God's dealing with man. They close off the age of the prophets and inaugurate the Church age, the age of the apostles (Mat. 19:28). In the Old Testament, it was the prophets who wrote scripture. In the New Testament, we find scripture being written by apostles. Christ in His earthly ministry never chose a prophet, a pastor, an evangelist, or a teacher. He chose apostles.

3. **The Post Ascension Apostles** - Ephesians 4 tells us that upon Jesus' ascension, He instituted yet another category of apostles. This is the group that is to be functioning throughout the church age or until "we all come in the unity of the faith, and of

the knowledge of the Son of God, unto a perfect man, unto the measure of the fullness of Christ" (Eph. 4:13). These apostles are part of the body of Christ, and if they are not functioning there will be a certain paralysis in the body (I Cor. 12:28). The New Testament mentions many apostles who fall into this category. Our list would include:

* Paul, Apostle to the Gentiles (Gal. 2: 7-8; Acts 9:15)
* Andronicus (Rom. 16:7)
* Junia(Rom. 16:7)
* James, the Lord's brother (Gal. 1:19)
* Barnabas (Acts 4:36; 14:14; 13:2)
* Titus(II Cor. 8:23)
* Epaphroditus (Phil. 2:25)
* Timotheos (I Thes. 1:1; 2:6)
* Silvanus (I Thes. 1;1; 2:6)
* Apollos (I Cor. 4:6, 9)

4. **Those Involved In Apostolic Type Ministry**
   In addition to the above categories, there seems to be quite a number of people in the New Testament, who did apostolic-type functions at times, who were never specifically called apostles. Probably the best examples of these are the seventy who Christ sent out to do basically what the twelve had done in previous experiences. This seems to answer the question about many in our day who have been instrumental in some apostolic work, but who do not appear to be specifically called to that ministry. There are many in this category in the body of Christ.

THE PREPARATION OF APOSTLES

God requires men to be fully prepared for the work in building His Church. The task of building God's House is the most important in all the world and God desires to use instruments that are well prepared. Second-rate spiritual instruments can only bring second-rate spiritual results. Too often in an individual's haste to get going in his ministry he wields an unskillful sword and thus does more harm than good. God will take every ministry through a time of preparation. Often the preparation will be long, but even in the natural realm, for someone who is going to handle delicate life and death matters (i.e. a brain surgeon), there is a long road of preparation.

God has a desire that those whom He would use in the ministry of the apostle have a good understanding of their weaknesses. Because of their influence over the lives of others, they are going to need deep humility. There are several examples in the Scriptures: Moses, Paul, Barnabas and Timothy.

Moses is an example of this in the Old Testament. God was going to use him to influence a large group of people, but first God had to work a deep humility in his spirit. Moses had great training and wisdom in terms of natural things, but God had to bring him to the place where he had no trust in any of it to accomplish the purposes of God.

Paul had a similar experience. Paul was a Pharisee with great learning and knowledge. Paul, like Moses, tried to fulfill his call in his own strength (Acts 9:23-31), but Paul was not ready yet. Just having a prophetic word over him was not enough. There was some preparation he had to go through. God had some true wisdom and understanding to build into him, and this would take time. He would need more than the gift of preaching. Paul received his call the day of his conversion, but he was not ready to be sent out for some time.

Barnabas was a man who was converted shortly after Pentecost. He was characterized as a selfless man from the time he began his walk with the Lord (Acts 4: 36-37). He yielded to the Lord and a submitted to God's delegated authority. As he continued in the Church at Jerusalem, he became a man of proven character. It is likely that he became one of the elders of the Jerusalem Church. About seven years after his conversion, he was sent to Antioch to strengthen the work there.

Timothy was also one who was prepared by God. He was raised in a godly home and was most likely converted to Christianity on Paul's first missionary journey through Lystra. He was familiar with the rejection that apostolic ministry could experience when he undoubtedly witnessed the stoning of Paul in that city. However, he proved his submission and obedience to the local leaders. As a result, when Paul came through the city a few years later, he was ready to begin preparing under the apostle Paul.

When these things are considered together, you find key attributes that apply to practically all who would be used in this ministry.

A. **The Intuition of a Call**-The initial stage of a personal apostolic calling for Paul came to him intuitively. He knew God was calling him as an apostle because God had shown it to him personally (Galatians 1:15). For any apostle in the making, the apostolic calling begins as an inner knowing or a spiritual sense that is clearly from God. This is just the beginning of a progressive out-working of the apostolic calling.

B. **The Intimation of a Call**-The next level of the personal calling Paul experienced came as an implication from Ananias just after Paul met Christ (note Acts 9:10-19). Jesus has told Ananias while he was in prayer that Paul was a chosen vessel. When Ananias prayed for Paul, he was filled with the Holy Spirit. It is clear that

Ananias shared this message from God with Paul, and though apostleship was not specifically mentioned, Paul's understanding that God was calling him was confirmed through another. Outside confirmation is an important key in the process of identifying and substantiating the apostolic call. Paul accepted the calling and began to pursue it from that day.

C. Indication of a Call-As time went on, the intuition and imitation of the call progressed to clear prophetic sanction. The best scriptural pattern we have for the process of selecting, ordaining, and setting legitimate apostles into office is the account of the prophetic gathering at Antioch. As the apostles prayed in Antioch, Paul and Barnabas were singled out by the voice of God as chosen instruments (Acts 13:2). This tells us that the appointment of apostles is a Spirit-led activity, that is done publicly and in a context of prayer and worship, and that several proven leaders need to agree.

To proceed in apostolic ministry without the keys of a prophetic, public and plural ordination by proven ministries would be entirely out of order in the emerging apostolic movement. Each candidate for the apostolic ministry must wait upon this kind of experience before pursuing the fullness of an apostolic call. In this way, many abuses and errors can be avoided. The apostolic networks put in place safeguards to ward against zealousness, lawlessness and anarchy.

D. The Impartation of the Call-The final confirmation of an apostolic calling came to Paul as hands were laid upon him in that same corporate gathering (Acts 13:2). Upon hearing what the Spirit was saying, God used the brethren at Antioch to impart blessing and anointing to Paul and Barnabas. Laying on of hands imparted divine power into the lives of these apostles and was the final seal upon their calling.

There is something else that seems to be a common experience among many of the apostles in the New Testament. Many apostles, it seems, were used of God in one of the other areas of the fivefold ministry. Paul, for example, was used as a teacher (Acts 11:25-26) before he was released to apostolic ministry. Peter seems to have had a pastoral emphasis in his ministry (John 21: 15-17; I Peter 5: 11-3). These other areas of function can be seen as preparatory in the life of the apostle, exposing him to avenues of ministry at home prior to his being sent out.

THE QUALIFICATIONS FOR AN APOSTLE

All of the governmental ministries must obviously qualify under the same list that applies to all elders (I Peter 5:1). Because of the special emphasis of each, however, there will also be qualities that should be strong in the lives of those called to each individual ministry. This is certainly true of the ministry of the apostle. In addition to the qualifications mentioned in relation to all elders, there are five qualities that should be very strong in one who desires the ministry of the apostles.

1. **AN APOSTLE** must have the heart of a father (I Cor.4:15; Phil.2:22). As a father he will nurture, admonish, nurse, cherish, and be gentle with God's people (Eph. 6:4; I Thess. 2: 6-8,11).

2. **AN APOSTLE** must have a deep love for and loyalty to the church of God. His love must be greater for the church than for his own ministry (I Cor.13).

3. **AN APOSTLE** must have patience (II Cor.

12:12). Because of his revelation and maturity it will be very easy for him to become impatient with the seemingly slow progress of those to whom he is ministering.

4. **AN APOSTLE** must not be given to self-glory (I Thess. 2:6; I Cor. 4: 9; II Cor. 10:8). He must not make people dependent on him; he must make them dependent on the Lord.

5. **AN APOSTLE** must have a servant's heart (Rom. 1:1; Phil. 1:1). The attitude of a servant is a supreme regard for the happiness and well-being of others. As a servant, an apostle should be characterized by humility, sacrifice and faithfulness (I Cor. 4: 9; II Cor. 10:18; 11: 22-23).

THE MINISTRY OF AN APOSTLE

When you study what was done by each of the apostles named in the Bible you find a great diversity of ministry. There are four different types of apostles: vertical apostles, horizontal apostles, hyphenated apostles, and marketplace apostles.

- **Vertical Apostles,** which is the most common, have authority over churches like Paul, Timothy and Titus (Titus 1:5, 12, 13- note the apostolic language).

- **Horizontal Apostles** can call together other apostles like James of Jerusalem, the brother of Jesus (Acts 15:6,13,19, 22, 28).

- **Hyphenated Apostles** have another primary function (e.g. Teacher-Apostle, Prophet-Apostle).

- **Market place Apostles** function mostly outside of the

structured church. They are in law, education, government, business, etc.

As you can see not all apostles do exactly the same thing, yet there are some things that seem to apply to most of those who fall into this category of apostle. The following points should help to summarize the ministry and work of the apostle:

1. The apostle will be involved in establishing churches on a proper foundation (I Cor. 3: 9-14; Eph. 2: 20; I Cor. 9: 1-2; 11: 34). This may involve developing new works or strengthening works already in existence (Rom.1:11; Col. 2: 5-7).

2. The apostle is one who will be particularly concerned about doctrinal exactness. (Acts 2:42; 15:1-31). Much of their work will depend on right doctrine.

3. The signs of an apostle accompany his ministry (Rom. 15: 18-19; II Cor. 12: 12).

4. The apostle may be involved in church discipline at times, particularly in relationship to the churches he has established (Acts 5: 1-11; II Cor. 5).

5. The apostle is involved in the ordination of ministries such as elders and deacons (Acts 6: 1-6; 14: 23; Tit. 1:5).

6. The apostle is involved in the feeding and training of other ministries (II Tim. 2:2). At times, this involves choosing workers and sending them to other churches and on special assignments (Acts 16: 1-4; Phil. 2: 19-25; Col. 4: 7-12).

7. The apostle is to be involved with caring for the churches which he has begun (II Cor. 1:28).

8. The apostle is used in the presbytery, in the laying on of hands and the impartation of spiritual gifts (I Tim.1: 18; 4: 14; II Tim. 1:6; Rom. 1:11).

9. The apostle is not a dictator (I Cor. 16:12), nor a lord over the sheep (I Pet. 5:2) As a father, he is to help the members of the body of Christ come to maturity (I Cor. 4: 15-16)

It can be easily seen from all this that the apostle has to have some capability to operate in all of the governmental ministries. As he goes into a new community, he will have to be able to do the work of an evangelist. As new converts come into the new church, he will have to be able to feed them and teach them in the ways of the Lord. As ministries mature, he will also have to serve as an example of the prophetic ministry.

THE RECOGNITION OF AN APOSTLE

God is vitally involved in every ministry that He has ordained. God in His sovereignty is the head over all and is responsible for several things in regard to a person's ministry. He determines the kind of ministry, the length of time the ministry functions, and the sphere of influence that the ministry is to have.

God calls the apostle. He determines how long he will minister and the kind of influence he will have. Not all apostles will be received as such by the body of Christ world-wide. Paul was not (I Cor. 9: 1-3) received by all. However, Paul knew where he was received and it was directly related to the places where he had produced apostolic fruit. It is possible for a man to be considered an apostle to one group, but not received as an apostle by another group.

The question remains, then, who should be recognized as an

apostle? An apostle should be recognized by at least four groups. First, he should know it himself. He should know God's call on his life. Second, he should be recognized by the local church leaders. A man's gift should be apparent to all. Third, he should be recognized by the people in his own church, having a good report throughout. Fourth, an apostle should be recognized by those he has grounded and established in the faith. Apart from this, an apostle needs no recognition except from God, for that is whom the apostle is ultimately serving.

THE OFFICE OF THE BISHOP

The Office of the Bishop

*I*n the New Testament Church, there are two offices designated and recognized by God, the bishop and the deacon. As we look at the office of the bishop in this study, we find that when we define the word, we automatically discover a great deal about the function of a New Testament bishop.

THE MEANING OF THE WORD

There are six main Greek word forms that shed light on this ministry in the Scripture. These words are familiar to us in their transliterated forms. However, in order for us to get correct, biblical view, we must look at their meanings in detail and see how they are used in the New Testament.

1. Presbuterion - This word literally means "assembly of aged men, or the order of elders." This term is used to refer to the council or senate among the Jews known as the Sanhedrin (Luke 22:66; Acts22:5), and it is used of the elders or bishops of a local Church (I Tim.4:14). At times the King James Version renders it presbytery" (I Tim. 4:14).

2. Presbuteros - This word simply means "elder, older person or a senior." At times this word simply refers to a person who

is advanced in years. He may be someone who is merely older than his peers or others around him (Luke 15: 25; John 8: 9). He may be a person who is advanced in life such as a senior citizen (Acts 2:17). In like manner, the feminine form may refer to older women (I Tim. 5:2).

At other times, this word is used in the New Testament to refer to the forefathers in Israel (Mat 15:2; Mk. 7: 3- 5; Heb. 11:2). All those listed in the "faith chapter" are referred to as elders.

The usage we are most concerned about in this context, however, is when this term is used to designate people of rank who are appointed officials of the people. Among the Jews this word had a general meaning, but it also had a specific meaning when it referred to members of local councils in individual cities (Josh. 20: 4; Ruth 4: 2), or members of a group of people in the Sanhedrin (Mat. 16:21; 26: 3; 27: 41). Among the early Christian churches this term was also used of official "leaders raised up and qualified by the Holy Spirit and appointed to have spiritual care of, and to exercise oversight over, the churches" (W.E. Vine).

3. Episkopos - This word means "an overseer, superintendent, guardian or bishop." It is a compound word in the Greek and comes from two words, the first being a preposition meaning "over" and the second a verb meaning..."to look or watch." Together they mean "to oversee" or "to watch over." This word is used five times in the New Testament (Acts 20: 28; Phil. 1: 1; I Tim. 3: 2; Titus 1: 7; I Pet. 2: 25).

4. Episkopeo - This is the verb form of episkopos and it means "exercising the oversight, to oversee, to care for, to look at, to take care of." It is used to express the kind of care we are to exercise over our own heart in "looking diligently" after our own inward condition (Heb. 12:15), it is used primarily in regard to the ministry of elders (I Pet.5: 2).

5. Episkopee - This word literally means "charge or care." It is

used for the position or office of an overseer (Acts 1: 2; I Tim. 3:1; also Num. 4:16).

6. Sumpresbuteros - This word is also a compound word. It is used only once in the New Testament by Peter who refers to those whom he is addressing as "fellow-elders" or "co-elders" (I Pet. 5:1).

A careful study of these words indicates that there is a close connection between the word elder and bishop; in fact, in the New Testament local church, they refer to the same office. The word bishop is a word that is descriptive of an office or a position, while the term elder refers to the stature and maturity of spiritual experience that the man who fills that office must possess. This close relationship of these terms is easily seen in general passages where both of these Greek words are used. Note the following verses where the Greek word used is in brackets behind the English rendering.

"And from Miletus he sent to Ephesus, and called the elders [presbuteros] of the church... Take heed therefore unto yourselves, and to all the flock, over which the Holy Ghost hath made you overseers [episkopos]" (Acts 20:17, 28).

"And ordain elders [presbuteros] in every city... for a bishop [episkopos] must be blameless" (Titus 1:5, 7).

The elders [presbuteros] which are among you I exhort ... feed the flock of God which is among you, taking the oversight [episkopos] thereof" (I Peter 5:2).

Shaff's Bible Dictionary describes it this way:
"In the New Testament, the term "bishop" is synonymous with presbyter or elder. Bishop is borrowed from the Greek and signifies the function. Presbyter is derived from an office in the synagogue and signifies the dignity of the same office. These presbyters or bishops of the apostolic period were the regular teachers, pastors,

and leaders of the congregation."

THE ORIGIN OF THE OFFICE

The office of the elder or bishop is first mentioned in Acts 11: 30 as if their function was clearly understood by all.

Perhaps the reason for this is that the office of the elder was not a new office at all. It was not new to the New Testament Church. It was, in fact, something that was very familiar to the people because it had been functioning for several hundred years. It was an office that was common to every synagogue.

Since this is the case, we can not look to the New Testament to find the origin of the office, we must look to the Old Testament. The first definition of the office of the elder comes under the ministry of Moses when first Jethro and later God, counseled him as to how to handle his people problem. It is important to have a good understanding of what took place in Israel's history because it seems that what God gave Moses, He also desired to be established in the local Church. The way God was to take care of the people problem was through plurality of oversight.

Moses' problem was that he was given oversight over more people than he could effectively handle. Not only was he sending himself to an early grave, but the people were becoming weary. As churches grow, every leader has to face this problem. It is a good problem, but a problem nonetheless, because if this problem is not handled properly God's work will not prosper. Into this situation came the counsel of Jethro (Exodus 18), and later the counsel of the Lord (Numbers 11) to set qualified men over the people to help Moses with the charge that God had placed on him.

There are patterns in the Old Testament regarding elders that will help us:

1. Elders were instituted as a matter of practical consideration. In Moses' situation the weight of the people had become more than he could bear. This is the same thing we see with the origin of deacons in Acts 6. There is no sense having an office

if there is no function to go with that office. A church needs as many elders as it takes to oversee the people effectively. A church of seventy-five does not need ten elders. The supply should be in a measure that is dictated by the demand.

2. Elders were always plural in number. Except for cases in the New Testament where a church had just started, all the churches eventually had plurality of eldership. In fact, there is no place in the New Testament where an established church is seen to have only one elder (Acts 11: 30; 14:23; 15: 2, 4, 6, 22, 23; 16: 4; 20: 17; 21: 18, etc).

3. Elders always had a specific function and charge. When elders are referred to in an official sense they always had a specific job description that demanded a good deal of their time and energy. They were not titular authorities; they were active, functioning leaders of the people.

4. The function of elders in the Old Testament seems to parallel that which was to come later in the New Testament Church.
   a. They were leaders in war.
   b. They were judges in disputes.
   c. They were men of good advice and counsel.
   d. They represented and maintained the community.
   e. They were the authorities of various cities.

5. It was necessary for elders to be in their place so that the people could find their place (Ex.18:23). Not only did the plurality of leadership make it possible for Moses to have an occasional day off, but the people also found their place. If every member of the local Church is going to find proper placement in the body it will take the ministry of more than one man (Eph. 4: 11-13).

"If thou shalt do this thing, and God command thee so, then thou shalt be able to endure, and all this people shall also go to their place in peace. So Moses hearkened to the voice of his father-in-law, and did all that he had said." Exodus 18:23-24

All through Israel's history they operated their political and religious affairs under the supervision of elders. Later when Israel did not have political autonomy they still maintained an eldership. During the Babylonian captivity the synagogue was established as a vehicle for keeping the people of God distinct in a strange land. Each synagogue had elders over it to guide, govern and instruct the people of God.

This pattern for eldership was operating in the synagogue in Jesus' day. This seems to be the pattern that Jesus had in mind for the Church. W.C. Hayden, in his book Church Polity, says:

"Elders among the Jews, were the rulers of the people, prominent men who took the lead in directing and controlling affairs. The elders of a city correspond to our councilmen, just as we now call them 'city fathers.' The elders of the people were their representatives and rulers in government and management of affairs pertaining to public welfare. As an official term therefore, this word expresses the idea of government by men of age, prominence, experience and wisdom. It indicates that this office is one that imposes important duties and grave responsibilities, and that it should be filled by men who are competent to perform the work devolving upon them efficiently and successfully. It indicates that an incompetent eldership is a great misfortune and disastrous in its consequences."

THE QUALIFICATIONS FOR BISHOPS AND ELDERS ARE THE SAME

God is very particular when it comes to choosing who is to oversee His House, because it is His House, and He wants to be the One who selects those who will rule over His House. In the economy of God, no one just decides to be an overseer. Every workman in God's House must be divinely called (Romans 1:1), for if a man is divinely called, he will also be divinely equipped. It takes supernatural enabling to be a New Testament overseer. Without this God-given equipment, no amount of preparation or schooling will do any good toward making men overseers. In fact, it does a great deal of harm when organizations ordain to leadership, men who are not called and equipped by God. Apart from being called and equipped by God, however, there are lists of qualifications that are given to us in the Word of God, to which an overseer must measure up. We find such lists in I Timothy 3: 1-7 and Titus 1:5-9. The New Testament does not put these qualifications forth as an ideal to strive for, but they are listed as the standards for all elders. These are qualifications that all elders/bishops MUST have (I Timothy 3:2). These cover moral, domestic and spiritual areas.

GOVERNMENT OF THE NEW TESTAMENT CHURCH BY ELDERSHIP

As we study Church government in the New Testament, it seems that the Divine intention is to have the "three-fold cord" of Church government (Eccl. 4: 12). This provides checks and balances in the government of any local church. For the sake of orderly thought, we will consider: The Chief Elder, The Multiple Eldership, and Congregational Representation (that may be the deacons).

1. The Chief Elder - First Among Equals

We submit this proposition for consideration. God's form of government is theocratic in character. This is to say, God chooses, calls and equips certain persons to be leaders and rulers over His people, investing and delegating them with degrees of authority according to His will. These persons are most commonly called "elders," and in any given group of elders, God generally places the mantle of leadership upon some one elder. This does not exalt this elder above the other elders, but sets him in responsibility as "first among equals."

Leadership in the Church is not arrived at by "the law of the jungle," i.e. "the survival of the fittest." This is not the way it is in the Kingdom of God. Jesus reproved the disciples for

their wrong motives and desire to exercise lordship and authority over the people as did the Gentiles (Luke 22: 24-27; I Peter
5:3). Christ Himself, as the risen Head of the Church, calls,
equips and places His mantle of leadership on that person to
lead the flock of God.

This person may be referred to as "bishop" or "chief elder"
or "senior pastor" or "senior minister" or "presiding elder,"
"apostle," etc. However, there must be leadership. Final deci-
sions for direction must be upon someone, otherwise there is
confusion, frustration and lack of direction for the people of
God.

2. Plurality of Eldership

Having seen that God does raise up leaders for His people
in "the set man," what then is the safeguard against this man
becoming a dictator or autocrat? What checks and balances
does the Lord provide to prevent a monarchial Bishop from
taking the pre-eminence as did Diotrephes (III John 9, 10)?

The answer is seen in the plurality (or multiple eldership)
and the co-equality of such persons. These checks and
balances are for the "chief elder" who is "first among equals."
He is first in leadership, but certainly not exalted above the
other elders.

Of the approximately 69 uses of the word "elder" in the
New Testament, twice it is used in a relational sense (Luke 15:
25; Romans 9:12), seven times it is used for an older person
and/or elder in an official sense (I Timothy 5: 1, 2, 19; I Peter
5: 1, 5; II John 1; III John 1), and about sixty times it is used in
an official sense in its plural sense.

The New Testament Church at Jerusalem, Antioch,
Philippi, Thessalonica and Ephesus all show plurality of eldership ministry and rule. Any given group of elders in a local
church at any given gathering of elders constitutes "the presbytery" at that place and time (I Tim. 4: 14). It is "elders" in
the plural and "church" in the singular when dealing with the
local church.

The wisdom of God is seen in the plurality of eldership because it:

    a. Safeguards a church from the rule of the one man or monarchial bishop.
    b. Provides checks and balances in rulership .
    c. Makes a channel for the manifold wisdom of God to be released to the Body of Christ, the Church.
    d. Provides multiple rule and feeding ministry in the local Church.
    e. Provides a covering and protection for all elders.

3. Co-Equality of Eldership

Not only does the Scriptures show us plurality of eldership, it also teaches the co-equality within that plurality of eldership. That is, no elder is to be exalted as a person above another elder. To do so is to violate God's own law and attitude toward His people, for God is no respecter of person (Romans 2: 11; Acts 10: 34; Deut. 10: 17; James 2: 1-9). He does not show partiality or favoritism.

The New Testament writers recognized and accepted both plurality and co- equality among the eldership. However, it is a co-equality of office and of elders as persons, but it is NOT a co-equality of divine ability.

There is a variety of personality, degrees of spirituality and measures of God given grace and ability within the eldership. They are all elders as persons, but there are differences of grace gifts given to them by the risen Head, Christ. Thus, all elders are equal as persons and office, but different in their grace-gifts, ability, responsibility, or spirituality.

Believers who see the plurality and co-equality of eldership in the Church often let the pendulum swing to extremes on this matter and fail to recognize that amongst this kind of eldership God does set some elders as " 'first among equals." The very fact that God has given a variety of ministry gifts, spiritual gifts, and talents to the members of the Body of Christ confirms the truth of the same among the eldership. It is this fact that should be seen in the example here of plurality and co-equality of eldership. Yet, an elder can be first among equals" by reason of divinely given abilities and grace.

THE SIMPLE DIFFERENCE

On a recent trip abroad a young man who carries the title Apostle asked me, to share with him the difference between an apostle and a bishop. My objective was to take what he was familiar with and draw several conclusions relative to the unknown.

To keep it simple, I asked him the following questions:

1. Would you agree that there is a difference between an elder and a pastor?
2. Would you also agree that there is a difference between an elder and a teacher or an evangelist?
3. Do you agree that a bishop is an elder, who is recognized as "first among his equals?"

If the answer to the last question is yes, then we can safely conclude that there is a difference between a bishop and a pastor, a bishop and a teacher, and a bishop and an evangelist, or a prophet, for that matter.

This sequence of question raised yet another question. **If a bishop is different from a prophet, an evangelist, a pastor and a teacher, wouldn't a bishop also be different from an apostle?** Basic deduction concludes that there is a difference.

To come to such a conclusion one has to believe that all of the ascension gifts of Christ listed in Ephesians 4 share equal, though different, purposes. Ephesians 4 does not provide a hierarchical listing; it simply presents a list of the five ascension gift ministries. In error, the Church has exaggerated some of the gifts, particularly that of the pastor and the evangelist. Even though it is listed fourth in Ephesians 4:11, the pastor is the most emphasized among churches. Likewise, denominations have ordained women as evangelist, even though the New Testament does not mention ordaining ascension gift ministries. It only speaks of ordaining elders and deacons.

As I read and understand Paul's writings in I Timothy 3 and in Titus 1, there are two offices of ordination. One is that of an elder, or those who qualify for the presbytery. The other is the office and the work of the deacon. In Acts 6:6, after the assembly selected the seven men who qualified according to the apostles' prerequisites, they presented them to the apostles for the laying on of hands and prayer. This was an act of ordination and setting aside for their participation in the administration of the first century church.

The point is that we must be careful how we create other works and office of ordination, like that of "evangelist" to keep from having to recognize women in ministry, or to set up a system of nothing more then a chain of command. Our God is a God of order, but He does not approve of systems that control and manipulate through the use of titles and positions. He alone is Lord. We have been admonished not to become lords over God's heritage. *Neither as being lords over God's heritage, but being ensamples to the flock.* I Peter 5:3(KJV)

GIFTS, ADMINISTRATIONS AND OPERATIONS

It is important for those of you who are serious about the subject of Apostles and Bishops, to accept the difference between the "works or gifts of Christ" and the "administration of Christ's work and ministry." Paul makes a clear distinction in I Corinthians 12 of the differences in the works and ministry of Christ, the gifts of the Spirit, and the works and operations of God, the Father.

> *Wherefore I give you to understand, that no man speaking by the Spirit of God calleth Jesus accursed: and that no man can say that Jesus is the Lord, but by the Holy Ghost.*
> *Now there are diversities of gifts, but the same Spirit. And there are differences of administrations, but the same Lord. And there are diversities of operations, but it is the same God which worketh all in all. But the manifestation of the Spirit is given to every man to profit withal.* I Corinthians 12:3-7(KJV).

"Gifts" in this text is the Greek word we're all familiar with "charisma" (Strongs Concordance 5486.) According to Vine's Dictionary, we come to the following definition:

Charisma- "a gift of grace, a gift involving grace" (charis) on the part of God as the donor, is used (a) of His free bestowments upon sinners, <Rom. 5:15,16; 6:23; 11:29>; (b) of His endowments upon believers by the operation of the Holy Spirit in the churches, <Rom. 12:6; 1 Cor. 1:7; 12:4,9, 28, 30,31; 1 Tim. 4:14; 2 Tim. 1:6; 1 Pet. 4:10>; (c) of that which is imparted through human instruction, <Rom. 1:11>; (d) of the natural "gift" of continence, consequent upon the grace of God as Creator, <1 Cor. 7:7>; (e) of gracious deliverances granted in answer to the prayers of fellow believers, <2 Cor. 1:11> (Vine's p. 284, 1997).

The ministry of Christ requires Christ's gifts. Christ's gifts to the body mentioned in Ephesians 4 are not charisma, but "domata."

Doma (SC1390), lends greater stress to the concrete character of the "gift," than to its beneficent nature, <Matt. 7:11; Luke 11:13; Eph. 4:8; Phil. 4:17> (Vine's p. 284, 1997).

The gifts of Christ (doma) are given for the purpose of doing Christ's ministry or works. These gifts endow the recipient to serve as Christ served or ministered.

MINISTERING, MINISTRATION, MINISTRY

Ministry

Diakonia (SC1248), "the office and work of a diakonos" (see MINISTER, A, No. 1), "service, ministry," is used (a) of domestic duties, <Luke 10:40>; (b) of religious and spiritual "ministration," (1) of apostolic "ministry," e. g., <Acts 1:17,25; 6:4; 12:25; 21:19; Rom. 11:13>, RV (KJV, "office"); (2) of the service of believers, e. g., <Acts 6:1; Rom. 12:7; 1 Cor. 12:5>, RV, "ministrations" (KJV, "administrations"); <1 Cor. 16:15; 2 Cor. 8:4; 9:1,12>, RV, "ministration"; <v. 13; Eph. 4:12>, RV, "ministering" (KJV, "the ministry," not in the sense of an ecclesiastical function); <2 Tim. 4:11>, RV, "(for) ministering;" collectively of a local church, <Acts 11:29>, "relief" (RV marg. "for ministry"); <Rev. 2:19>, RV, "ministry" (KJV, "service"); of Paul's service on behalf of poor saints, <Rom. 15:31>; (3) of the "ministry" of the Holy Spirit in the gospel, <2 Cor. 3:8>; (4) of the "ministry" of angels, <Heb. 1:14>, RV, "to do service" (KJV, "to minister"); (5) of the work of the gospel, in general, e. g., <2 Cor. 3:9>, "of righteousness; "<5:18>, "of reconciliation"; (6) of the general "ministry" of a servant of the Lord in preaching and teaching, <Acts 20:24; 2 Cor. 4:1; 6:3; 11:8; 1 Tim. 1:12>, RV, "(to His) service"; <2 Tim. 4:5>; undefined in <Col. 4:17>; (7) of the Law, as a "ministration" of death, <2 Cor. 3:7>; of condemnation, <3:9> (Vines, p. 445, 1997).

When it comes to the operations of God, the Bible is referring to the source of power, energy or effectiveness needed to do the work we have been assigned. This speaks to callings.

> *Whereof I was made a minister, according to the gift of the grace of God given unto me by the effectual working of his power (*Ephesians 3:7 KJV).

> *Whereunto I also labour, striving according to his working, which worketh in me mightily (*Colossians 1:29 KJV).

The word "operation" is rendered "working." Let's examine it.

Working

1. Energeia (SC1753), (Eng., "energy") is used (1) of the "power" of God, (a) in the resurrection of Christ, <Eph. 1:19; Col. 2:12>, RV, "working" (KJV, "operation"); (b) in the call and enduement of Paul, <Eph. 3:7; Col. 1:29>; (c) in His retributive dealings in sending "a working of error" (KJV, "strong delusion") upon those under the rule of the Man of Sin who receive not the love of the truth, but have pleasure in unrighteousness, <2 Thes. 2:11>; (2) of the "power" of Christ (a) generally, <Phil. 3:21>; (b) in the church, individually, <Eph. 4:16>; (3) of the power of Satan in energizing the Man of Sin in his "parousia," <2 Thes. 2:9>, "Coming."#

2. Energema (SC1755), "what is wrought," the effect produced by No. 1, occurs in <1 Cor. 12:6>, RV, "workings" (KJV, "operations"); <v.10 (Vine's, p.777, 1997).

Effectiveness and efficiency speak to ones qualifications and readiness. These are the considerations of those who select men and women from among the assembly to become those who work as ministers, deacons, elders and bishops in the Lord's church. No presbytery can qualify you to receive the gifts of Christ; it is determined by God. Man cannot make you an apostle, a prophet, an evangelist, a pastor, or a teacher. Though men may name or nominate you to any of these ascension gift offices, there will be no anointing to function as such, if God has not ordained it. Ephesians 4:11, says that "HE gave some." The Bible gives us patterns, but not qualifications to determine one's ability to be an apostle, prophet, evangelist, pastor, or teacher. What we can do as the church is recognize gifts according to the patterns we have been given, and measure the effectiveness based on the grace given to perform in that capacity. We can look at it anthropomorphically by examining the hands of God.

THE HANDS OF GOD

If God is known in the earth, He is made known according to His presentation to man. We see God throughout scripture presented with the same physical attributes that men have. We read about the hands of God, the eyes of the Lord, the touch of the Lord, etc. If God in His presentation of Himself to man is made like man, we can conclude that He has two hands. This is referenced in the following scriptures.

Num 11:23

And the LORD said unto Moses, Is the LORD's hand waxed short? thou shalt see now whether my word shall come to pass unto thee or not. (KJV)

Josh 4:24

That all the people of the earth might know the hand of the LORD, that it is mighty: that ye might fear the LORD your God for ever. (KJV)

Acts 11:21

And the hand of the Lord was with them: and a great number believed, and turned unto the Lord. (KJV)

Exod 15:6

Thy right hand, O LORD, is become glorious in power: thy right hand, O LORD, hath dashed in pieces the enemy. (KJV)

Job 23:9

On the left hand, where he doth work, but I cannot behold him: he hideth himself on the right hand, that I cannot see him: (KJV)

The Hands of God work in His Church to make it an organized organism. This is not intended to be a lesson on the post ascension gifts of Christ, but a presentation of how He works in the Body with both hands. I present this as the Lord has given it to me. On the right hand, we will find "The Ministry Gifts of Christ." On the left hand, we find "The Operations or Workings of Christ's Ministry, in the Body."

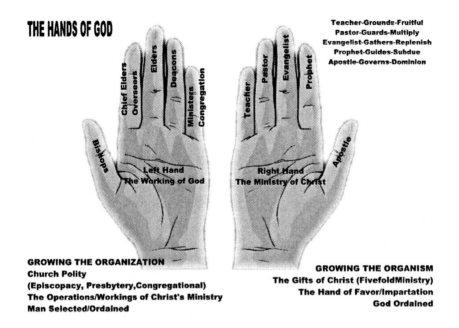

THE HANDS OF GOD

Teacher-Grounds-Fruitful
Pastor-Guards-Multiply
Evangelist-Gathers-Replenish
Prophet-Guides-Subdue
Apostle-Governs-Dominion

Chief Elders
Overseers
Elders
Deacons
Ministers
Congregation
Bishop

Teacher
Pastor
Evangelist
Prophet
Apostle

Left Hand
The Working of God

Right Hand
The Ministry of Christ

GROWING THE ORGANIZATION
Church Polity
(Episcopacy, Presbytery,Congregational)
The Operations/Workings of Christ's Ministry
Man Selected/Ordained

GROWING THE ORGANISM
The Gifts of Christ (FivefoldMinistry)
The Hand of Favor/Impartation
God Ordained

If these hands do nothing else, they show us that God uses both hands in his ministry and workings of the Church. We can also see that the "bishop" and the "apostle" are on separate hands. They are not the same; however, they do work together. Both are significant. One can be both a bishop and an apostle; a bishop and a pastor; a bishop and a prophet; a bishop and an evangelist; or, a bishop and a teacher.

Likewise, a person can be an elder and an apostle; an elder and a prophet; an elder and an evangelist; an elder and a pastor; or, an elder and a teacher. If a presbytery has never selected a person and set them aside in any of the fivefold gifts, the individual must yet qualify according to the pattern of these gifts and the qualifications for eldership, which speak to maturity. For example, we may have people in our congregations without titles who are gifted by Christ to carry on His work of "perfecting the saints, for the work of ministry, for the edifying of the body." Being overlooked or unrecognized by man, does not cancel the ministry gift for which you have been predestined.

Frequently, the system in the church leaves many gifts dormant and latent. There are prophets waiting to prophesy in churches that don't believe that prophecy is biblical. There are apostles in churches who have been silenced because of the unbelief of leaders in denominations. These apostles are waiting to be released to bring the body to a place of order and "full measure." To those apostles who have been silenced, I speak to you, "That time is of the essence. Others await your gift. It's time to shift!"

POSITION STATEMENT

Position Statement

We cannot allow our old ways to create for us a miosis on the subject of Apostles and Bishops. The order of the Lord is being restored to His Church. Because the Church has been out of order on many issues, the order of God challenges us to recognize, accept and adopt truth that displaces and replaces what traditionally we received as true and correct. To adopt things that we have historically rejected or denied requires humility and submission to the way of God, while at the same time being subjected to some possible humiliation. The spiritual enzyme or catalyst that's needed to make these changes is "a heart for God." You've got to want God and what God wants more than anything!

1. Bishops were never meant to be hierarchical offices in the church. They were not purposed by God to be "rulers" over his people. They were only intended to be the "first elder" among his equals. To that extent, you could possibly find one in every church! Just as the size of the church should determine the number of elders needed, the number of elders should determine if a "chief elder," or "overseer," or a "bishop" is needed.

2. Apostles can be treated no differently than the other four ministry gifts of Ephesians 4:11. Each of the five-fold ascension gift ministries represents one-fifth part (20%) of Christ's mantle in the earth. Wherever either is missing, the perfecting of the saints cannot result. To take on Christ's mantle in the earth requires maturity. You cannot be a neophyte. Elders are

categorically mature, divinely gifted leaders. These are the persons who should be ordained to the five-fold ministry work. Others who have obvious giftings, but not maturity, may be used of the Lord as given to us in I Corinthians 12, but should not be ordained or set apart in the office.

3. The correct way to release people into five-fold gift ministry is:

A. To ordain him or her as an elder based on the moral, domestic and spiritual qualifications in I Timothy 3 and Titus 1.

B. To affirm them as elders who serve in the "office" of Apostle, Prophet, Evangelist, Pastor or Teacher.

This would correct how we have historically labeled certain gifts, i.e., "evangelists" who we have not elevated to a place of ordination.

Thus, ordained elders should be properly affirmed by 1) the congregation, 2) their peers, and 3) those to whom they are submitted for accountability.

They may afterward be referred to by the "office" they primarily operate in for Body identification, but NOT for the establishing of any hierarchy or personal glory from the title. It should be okay to be called elder, or brother, etc.

4. "Apostles" and "Bishops" are not synonymous works, though in all cases an apostle will perform the work of the bishop. Reason being, his mantle sets him as "first" in the church. Likewise, the bishop is "first among his equals."

However, I believe "bishops" may have other five-fold ministry ascension gifts. To say it differently, there are elders, who are first among their equals, in each of the five-fold ministry offices. There are bishops with the gift of "teacher" or "pastor" or "evangelist" or "prophet" as well as the "apostle." Yet, when all of these "headship" ministries flow together in the Body, the bishop in the office of the "apostle" would be first among his equals.

5. Since both bishops and five-fold ascension gift ministries are "elders" in the church, the one office that reflects "first among equals" must be the key reflection of the "chief" office that would be bishop. So to be "promoted" from a Bishop to an Apostle, as many are now doing, is out of order.

The truth is, that person probably has been operating as an Apostle for some time. When he's recognized as "first among many," he should be affirmed as a "bishop" who serves the Body as a "Bishop-Apostle" or "Chief Apostle." This is not elevation; it's identification for effective service. He does not suddenly go to another level; he becomes first among other apostles. This does not become a title, but the work of his office.

6. It's also noteworthy that the five-fold ascension gift ministries are spiritual endowments from God; He chooses who will be gifted to walk in an office. The New Testament selections of the bishop/elder and deacon are made by the church. We are given, for the bishop and deacon, criteria by which the church can determine the readiness of the candidate. No such criteria are provided for five-fold ministry. We can only judge their works by biblical pattern and prayerful application of hermeneutics. The rest, God will have to set in order when He comes.

7. If the integrity of the first century church is maintained, the office of the "bishop" must be seen as local. If we allow 21st Century revelation to effect us, he may also be a "bishop" to trans-local elders who have submitted themselves to his leadership. The "apostle" (as well as the other fivefold gifts) are given to the Body at-large (trans-local) inasmuch as these are headship gifts that keep Christ active in the Church.

Printed in the United States
20627LVS00001B/448-828